if you've ever loved a married man

by one who did

Published by

dune

Publications Ltd.

47-25 59th St.
Woodside, N.Y. 11377

FIFTH PRINTING
ISBN 0-914938-02-9
Library of Congress Catalog Number 74-17596

Manufactured in the United States of America
by P&S Graphics Ltd., New York, N.Y.

Sketches by George Thune

. . . and dammit still does

This book is dedicated for those like me . . .
    . . . who thought it would work.

It is not a diary, nor a collection of loving poems.
It is a bound assortment of confused emotions.

PROLOGUE

Love makes you
susceptible.

Like being a little duck
in a shooting gallery.
You can't dodge the bullets.
So each time you go down
you pick yourself up again.
But every hit leaves
a small dent . . .

Go . . .
bring me a balloon . . .
if it's not
too heavy . . .

I

**ONCE I WENT OUT
CHASING RAINBOWS. . .**

1.

I love a man
who is half mine
half the time . . .
he can't let me
into his world
so I tip-toe
to the fence
trying to
peek in . . .
he dug a hole
under the fence
so that he could
come see me . . .

he needs love . . .
so I wait
outside for him . . .
and I need
this man
who is
half mine
half the time . . .

2.

I know you . . .
where you're ticklish . . .
looks of approval . . .
I like to make you
feel like a kid
and your
favorite dessert . . .
and if I could
make a present of
the world in
bite-size pieces
you would have it
peeled and sliced . . .

3.

There are none better . . .
just great virile statues
slouching
in practiced postures . . .
just revolving-door
reflections
posing . . .
in oh-so-perfect stances . . .
you are real . . .
I
love you . . .

4.

**An
extraordinary sensation
you . . .
a
fantastic find
us . . .**

5.

You should stay over
more often . . .
I like scrambling eggs
for you . . .
and helping you dress . . .
and the bathroom
always smells like
your no-occasion presents . . .

6.

Maybe I care too much
and worry when a smile
is missing from
your face . . .
and I touch you
too often . . .
maybe any words
I can think of
would sound
so stupid . . .

7.

Do I sometimes
fall short
of your expectations . . .
I'm sorry for any word
I ever left out . . .
or any embrace
I ever forgot . . .

8.

When I do things
for you
they always seem
so small in comparison . . .
I want to do
bunches of things
to make you
happy . . .
like get you a guarantee
that said
you'd never get caught
in the rain . . .

or a life-time
insurance policy
that promised
you'd never need
a band-aid . . .
and I'd make sure
no one would ever
run out
of your
favorite ice cream . . .

and you'd always
have someone to
brag to
or cry to
when you need to . . .
and no hurt could
ever touch you . . .
I'll give you
love
in the bad times
for the good times
couldn't be
made happier . . .

9.

Remember that weekend . . .
I needed a rest
and you loaned me
some money . . .
like you always do . . .
it was cold outside
watching our stars
winking
at disinterested trees . . .
I wanted to rip one out
and watch the
sky bleed . . .

you were one night away
but I sent a postcard
disguising my hand-writing . . .
and I wished like hell
I could complain about
your loud snoring . . .

10.

Away from you
I learned
that away from you
is too difficult . . .
because there is
nothing baby
more perfect
than us
for us . . .

11.

Can you believe . . .

that I still get goose-bumpy
making little surprises for you . . .

that I'm more afraid than ever
that you'll go . . .

that we're never short
of smiles . . .

that we crammed so much life
and so much love
into 365 days . . .

12.

Press your thirsty mouth
against me
I'll feed you all you
need . . .
ask . . . ask . . . ask . . .

II

ONCE I WENT OUT
CHASING RAINBOWS . . .
AND TRIPPED OVER
A POT OF GOLD . . .

13.

Funny how
one telephone ring
meant . . .
hi . . .
I'm thinking of you . . .
I love you . . .
I'm fine . . .
I hope you are . . .
wish I was with you . . .
talk to you tomorrow . . .
goodnight . . .
and I never
lifted the receiver.

14.

Nightmares about
losing each other . . .
and it's almost
two years since
love
punched us in the gut . . .

almost two years' worth
of deceit . . .
you kidding her . . .
me kidding
myself . . .
loving you . . .
hating the
lies . . .

and we keep wishing
things could be
different . . .
rotting away
half happy . . .
knowing we should
know better . . .

going neither
forward
nor
backward . . .
you're a
coward . . .
as I . . .

15.

I was almost sorry
for asking you
to stay . . .
awaking to the
sound of
whispered excuses
on my
kitchen extension . . .

sure they have
to be made . . .
but why did you
sound
so
apologetic . . .

16.

The sound of the water faucet
means you'll be
leaving soon . . .
you always wash the
love off . . .
leaving no traces
of where
you've been . . .

rushing to where
the bed
has been warmed
for you . . .
telling me
how bad you feel
while you put
your socks on . . .
I'm having
trouble
living with
or without you . . .

17.

I'd pack
my paranoia
and leave . . .
but I need you . . .
leave your
toothbrush . . .
we'll have our
laughs . . .

we can drink
iced coffee and
play house . . .
until I'm
too exhausted
to play . . .
or until the
flowers
stop coming . . .

18.

All the
advice of
concerned friends . . .
watching me
crumble . . .
knowing how
truly lucky
and
unhappy
I am . . .
can't matter . . .

19.

Did she notice
the pizza stain
on your tee shirt . . .
or the dog hairs
on the bottom
of your socks . . .

20.

All right . . .
your life doesn't
center around me . . .
damn it . . .
you're my whole show . . .
look up
wave sometimes . . .
it gets lonely
watching from
the bleachers . . .
even though
I have a
reserved seat . . .

21.

There are just
certain people
you can introduce
me to . . .
and I can't get
mascara
on your shirt collar . . .

22.

Trying to
accept
a half
existence . . .
often
I think
you're worth it . . .
how unfortunate . . .
she
agrees . . .

23.

Shop-lifting cigarettes
and mock rape scenes . . .
all the
temporary fantasies . . .
but you get dressed
so soon
and come and go
like a
telephone repairman . . .

24.

Saying
I love you . . .
in coded words . . .
ringing
my phone once
when she's
near and you
can't talk . . .
while I
compete
with an
unknown rival . . .

25.

Is it Sunday already . . .
the day you play
Mr. and Mrs. America . . .
re-meet all your
relatives . . .
and grandma coddles
a slightly-big-for-his-age
grandson . . .

26.

What kind of
magnet
is she . . .
really . . .
to keep you
running back . . .

27.

Stay, have some
hot chocolate . . .
it'll hold you
a little longer . . .
then say you'll be
back real soon
so I have something
to stick around for . . .

28.

It's five days
you've been in bed
but not mine . . .
and there's no way
I can help . . .
except to try and
sound cheerful
when you sneak
me a call
to say how bad
you feel . . .
and there's no way
I can help . . .

29.

Not so simple . . .
the classic
crap . . .
he meets she . . .
dumps other she . . .
carries off
new she . . .

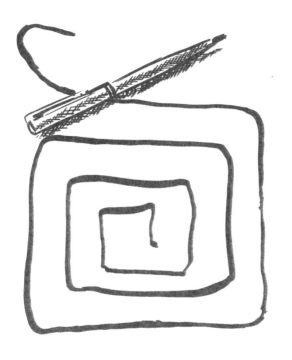

30.

I can't pretend
I didn't know
where you'd be . . .
holidays . . .
while I was being my own
Easter Bunny . . .
sang Jingle Bells
solo . . .

screamed happy new year
at a black and white t.v. . . .
and there's no place
like home . . .

31.

Does each day
really
bring another
chance . . .
or does it
merely compound
mistakes
from the
day before . . .

32.

We must all do
something a
first time . . .
and if the
pain was worth it . . .
we will
punish ourselves
from force of
habit . . .

33.

Why is it
people would rather
coax you into
a plastic smile . . .
than try to
understand
an
honest frown . . .

III

ONCE I WENT OUT
CHASING RAINBOWS. . .
AND TRIPPED OVER
A POT OF GOLD . . .
AND
STUBBED MY TOE . . .

34.

I knew
you weren't
happy at home . . .
now
I know
you're not
uncomfortable . . .

35.

There's been
a transition . . .
from happy
lover . . .
to
unhappy husband
cheating . . .

quite accustomed
to walking out . . .
expecting my world
to stop
when yours does . . .
forgetting I need to be
needed . . .
screwing takes no
special talent . . .

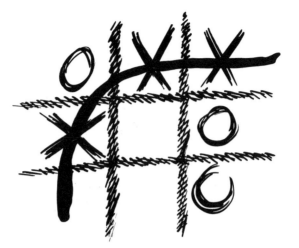

36.

Being married . . .
excuses much neglect . . .
best of both worlds
you cheat two women . . .
I resent
borrowed smiles
and
second-hand tenderness . . .

37.

I've stood so often
in the sidelines
anonymously admiring you . . .
we forgot
we both were
competing
for the spotlight . . .

38.

I know I can make you
happier
than you've ever been . . .
I did once . . .
but you're a creature
of habit . . .
squeezing me into
your
spare seconds . . .

39.

You could give
me up
the way you would
smoking . . .
and the ugly me
is showing . . .
the me
that needs to
feel important
too . . .

while a
two-year-old
villain
with smiling freckles
holds my future
in his fist . . .
a two-legged
cherub
with a bubble-gum
giggle . . .
Hi Daddy . . .

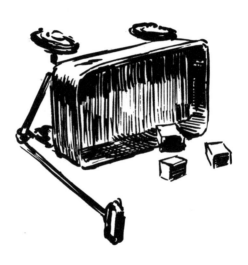

when you call
from home . . .
I can hear his
little-person-voice
behind yours . . .
it's good
that toys
are his only
preoccupation . . .

40.

I'm beginning
to feel much
like a condemmed
building . . .
whose guts are
nailed shut . . .
for fear
of being
too real
a reminder . . .

while the one treasure
I prize so jealously . . .
kisses me lovingly
and
leaves . . .
before my eyes
have re-opened . . .

commuting
into my life . . .
waiting
for some
magic answer . . .
waking to a
woman he
doesn't love . . .
leaving me
a set of
headphones . . .
that are
no substitute . . .

41.

I used to nurse your colds
and help pick ties
for shirts we bought . . .
I used to feel
a little special . . .
now I'm just
reserved . . .

42.

You stampeded into
my life . . .
and I've become
a deduction on your
expense account . . .

43.

Happy Birthday Darling . . .
it always means a
celebration
either the day before
or the day after . . .
and presents that will be
tucked
into my dresser drawers . . .

and the best kind of gift
is something she'd believe
you bought for yourself . . .
in case you wear it home
by mistake . . .

44.

All our snapshots are
stashed in drawers . . .
someday I'll paste
them up . . .
and show my friends
all the places
I've been
with someone else's
husband . . .

45.

Even the
pizza
delivery man . . .
thinks
we're a pair . . .

46.

I can't
vomit you
out of the past . . .
and the future
promises
large lonely gaps . . .

47.

How do you segregate
what we had . . .
into mine and yours . . .
I sorted some things
into brown paper bags . . .
pick them up
when you have
somewhere else
to leave them . . .

48.

I love
you love
he, she, it loves
we love
you love
they love
I love
you love

RETROSPECT...

AT THE END OF
THE RAINBOW

Packing brings
so many
sentimental pangs . . .
special words with
special meanings . . .
and hurts that
always seemed to
get better . . .

There were moments . . .
we were good . . .
more than is
believable . . .
but knowing there's
a whole pie
in the window
when all you're
handed is
a skimpy slice . . .

makes you think
that's all
you're worth . . .
until someone
else
sledge-hammers home
the truth . . .

I've bundled up
what little pride
you left me . . .
realizing
you didn't want
love . . .
you wanted
applause . . .

And the memory
of those
counterfeit encounters . . .
well,
you just needed me
to
tide you over . . .

But,
I doubt I'll ever
laugh so hard
or cry so loud
again.

reasons for leaving

- [ ] too many lies
- [ ] can't share him anymore
- [ ] another lonely sunrise
- [ ] he spent Christmas with her
- [ ] too many arguments
- [ ] waiting for his calls
- [ ] going to parties alone
- [ ] his kiss goodnight
- [ ] because....

reasons for staying

- ☐ so many laughs
- ☐ half is better than none
- ☐ the sunshine in his eyes
- ☐ Valentine's Day roses
- ☐ the weekend we stole
- ☐ his sometime whispers
- ☐ the poem he wrote me
- ☐ his kiss goodnight
- ☐ because....

more reasons for leaving....

more reasons for staying....

afterthoughts....

afterthoughts....

afterthoughts....

afterthoughts....

afterthoughts....

afterthoughts....

OTHER POETRY BOOKS PUBLISHED BY

Publications Ltd.

*"POTENT"   *"ACHIEVES EXCELLENCE"
*"GREAT"   *"TENDER"

the sadness of happy times

by lou duro

WITH A
SPECIAL
INTRODUCTION
BY
HERB OSCAR
ANDERSON

* "This is a book of GOOD POETRY; a continuous story of a love affair, really, and many of the pieces, taken as individual, abstract works, approach or ACHIEVE EXCELLENCE... If you liked 'Love Story', YOU'LL LOVE, 'THE SADNESS OF HAPPY TIMES'...demands the attention of every admitted incurable romantic and more than a notice from many of the rest of us who hesitate to admit we are."
—MICHAEL O'NEIL

* "POTENT VOLUME OF LOVE POEMS which will find sympathetic echoes in your heart — perhaps almost too painful if you are newly fallen out of love... With simplicity and gentleness, Duro traverses the varied experiences of our search for ideal love — the expectancy, the eager grasping of each tender moment, the highs when we feel sure that this is it, the heartbreak of love lost."
—CHARLOTTE AMES

* "After reading, 'The Sadness of Happy Times', I know that LOU DURO IS A GREAT POET."
—JOHN BARTHOLOMEW TUCKER

* "If you have ever been in love and been hurt... READ 'THE SADNESS OF HAPPY TIMES'. Lou Duro tenderly puts into a few words what you have been trying to say all this time."
—DAN DANIEL
RADIO PERSONALITY

MAIL TO:

Publications Ltd.

47-25 59th Street
Woodside, N.Y. 11377

PLEASE SEND ME _____ COPIES OF the sadness of happy times by lou duro AT $3.95 EACH (Plus 60 cents postage and handling) MY CHECK (or money order) FOR $ _____ IS ENCLOSED.

MAKE PAYABLE TO DUNE PUBLICATIONS LTD.
Please print clearly

Name _____

Address _____

City _____ State _____ Zip _____